OUR
AMERICA

GROWING UP IN A NEW CENTURY

1890 TO 1914

JUDITH PINKERTON JOSEPHSON

Judith Pinkerton Josephson

Lerner Publications Company
Minneapolis

In memory of my father-in-law, Donald V. Josephson

Thanks to Kirsten Josephson, Edith Fine, Marissa West, Melissa Irick, Stephanie McPherson, my critique group, and the Fisher family—Mary Catherine, Ona, Amy, William, and Abby. I am also grateful to Jan Spreeman, Pat Hatfield, the Minnesota Historical Society, the Blue Earth County Historical Society, the Virginia Historical Society, and the Library of Congress. For her vision for this series and for her careful editing, thanks to my editor, Sara Saetre.

Lerner Publications Company
A division of Lerner Publishing Group
241 First Avenue North
Minneapolis, MN 55401 U.S.A.

Website address: www.lernerbooks.com

Photographs and illustrations in this book are used with the permission of: Kansas Collection, University of Kansas Libraries, p. 5; Missouri Historical Society, Worlds Fair #862, p. 6; Courtesy of Judith and Kirsten Josephson, pp. 7, 12, 25, 32, 44; © North Wind, pp. 8, 42 (both), 46, 49, 50, 55, 56, 57; Cincinnati Museum Center, p. 10; Laura Westlund, map pp. 10–11; Schlesinger Library, Radcliffe College, p. 13; L. Frank Baum Papers/The George Arents Research Library for Special Collections at Syracuse University, p. 14; Theodore Roosevelt Collection, Harvard College Library, p. 16; The Granger Collection, p. 17; Brown Brothers, p. 19; Smithsonian Institution Photo No. 56095, p. 20; Courtesy of the Rockefeller Archive Center, p. 21; © Bettmann/CORBIS, pp. 22, 26; University of Illinois at Chicago, the University Library, Jane Addams Memorial Collection, p. 23; Brigham Young University, p. 24; National Archives, neg # 102-LH-1056, p. 27; Library of Congress, pp. 28, 29, 30; Colorado Historical Society, p. 31; © H. Armstrong Roberts/CORBIS, p. 34; © CORBIS, pp. 37, 41, 54; Florida State Archives, p. 38; Beltrami County Historical Society, p. 39; Denver Public Library, Western History Department, p. 40; Jim Simondet/IPS, p. 43; Archive Photos, p. 45; Minnesota Historical Society, pp. 48, 59; © Araldo de Luca/CORBIS, p. 51; University Settlement Archives, p. 52.
Front cover image: © Minnesota Historical Society/CORBIS

Library of Congress Cataloging-in-Publication Data

Josephson, Judith Pinkerton.
    Growing Up in a New Century, 1890 to 1914 / by Judith Pinkerton
Josephson.
        p.   cm. — (Our America)
    Includes bibliographical references (p.) and index.
    Summary: Presents details of daily life of American children during
the period from 1890 to 1914.
    ISBN: 0–8225–0657–2 (lib. bdg. : alk. paper)
    1. United States—History—1865–1921—Juvenile literature.
2. United States—Social life and customs—1865–1918—Juvenile
literature. 3. Children—United States—Social life and customs—
19th century—Juvenile literature. 4. Children—United States—
Social life and customs—20th century—Juvenile literature.
5. United States—History—1865–1921—Sources—Juvenile
literature. [1. United States—Social life and customs—1865–1918.
2. United States—History—1865–1921.] I. Title. II. Series.
E661.J84 2003
973.91'092'2—dc21   2001006827

Manufactured in the United States of America
1 2 3 4 5 6 – JR – 08 07 06 05 04 03

Contents

Note
to
Readers

Studying history is like detective work. Historians gather clues about the past by studying old diaries, letters, magazines, and photographs. All these things are primary sources.

While writing this book, the author used many primary sources. She snooped into life in the United States at the turn of the last century, from about 1890 to about 1914. Many things were different from modern times. For example, some youngsters had to work underground all day long, almost never seeing the sun. Luckier children enjoyed rides in the first automobiles and attended the first high schools.

As this photograph shows, youngsters at the turn of the last century often wore dressy clothes even when playing sports or going fishing. These boys are wearing short pants called knickers. The photograph they are taking is a primary source.

Many books about history are really historical fiction. Historical fiction is a made-up story that is set in a real time. In this book, the people you will meet are real. You'll see photographs of them and read quotes from their diaries and letters. The quotes are printed here just the way they were written, misspellings and all.

By studying the primary sources in this book, you'll have a chance to do some detective work of your own. Your ideas about the past will add to our understanding of people, especially youngsters, who watched the 1900s begin.

CHAPTER ONE

The Children's Hour

"The World is so full of a number of things, I'm sure we should all be happy as kings."

—from "Happy Thought" by Robert Louis Stevenson, 1913

"Starlight, moonlight, I hope to see my ghost tonight," shouted five-year-old Mary Wigginton. Giggling, she ran behind the lilac bushes. Mosquitoes whined. Crickets chirped their nighttime chorus. Mary's brother Frank was "It." He put his hands over his eyes and counted: "Six, seven, eight, nine, ten! Here I come, ready or not!" The Wigginton children were playing "starlight, moonlight," a hide-and-seek game. They lived in Saint Paul, Minnesota, in the early 1900s.

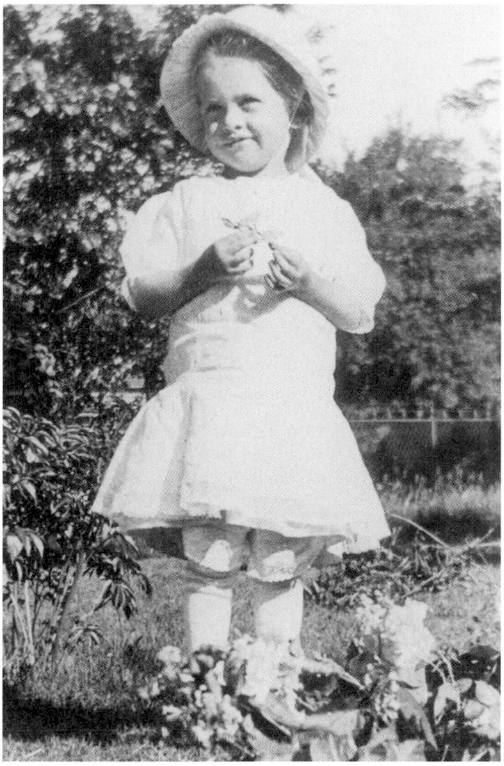

Opposite: Ice cream cones were a newly invented treat when this photograph was taken in 1904 at the World's Fair in Saint Louis, Missouri. *Above:* Mary Wigginton in the early 1900s

A New Frontier

The 1900s (also called the twentieth century) brought big changes for American children. In the 1800s, pioneers had pushed into America's "Wild West." But by 1900, the West had largely been settled. Big cities such as New York, New York, and Chicago, Illinois, were the new American frontier.

Cities like these bustled with thousands of immigrants who streamed into the United States from other countries. Factories churned out clothes, bread, and other things that people had once made at home. People ordered bicycles, shoes, and even houses from the Sears, Roebuck, & Co. Catalog, the "Cheapest Supply House on Earth."

New inventions such as the telephone were changing people's lives. The first telegraph message crossed the Atlantic Ocean in 1900. Electric lights made big cities glow. Indoor bathrooms (also called water closets) appeared, making it easier to bathe regularly. "Cleanliness is next to godliness" became a popular saying.

Horses still pulled buggies that hauled around people and goods. But some people drove automobiles, another new invention. In 1900 Americans owned only eight thousand automobiles (nicknamed jalopies, tin lizzies, or horseless carriages). By 1910 Americans had nine million cars.

Sometimes young people had to teach their parents how to handle these new contraptions. In 1908 George Anderson tried to teach his father how to drive a Model T Ford. When Mr. Anderson wanted to stop the car, he shouted, "Whoa!" The car rolled into a tree. Mr. Anderson stuck to horses after that.

> *When Mr. Anderson wanted to stop the car, he shouted, "Whoa!"*

Just as some modern youngsters show older people how to use computers, some youngsters in the early 1900s taught their parents how to handle this new invention, the automobile.

DEAR DIARY

On December 31, 1899, farmboy George Anderson wrote that the last day of the 1800s was "very cold" in Marine-on-Saint Croix, Minnesota. George took a walk anyway to "walk the old year out and the new one in."

Children of this era didn't have TVs, VCRs, or computers. But many kept diaries. They wrote about everyday doings, holidays, and vacations. On a family vacation in 1898, eleven-year-old Sarah Baylor visited the historic Washington Monument in Washington, D.C. "Margaret and I counted the steps from the top of the monument to the bottom," Sarah told her diary. "There are 1000."

Young people also wrote about historic events. When the American battleship *Maine* exploded near Cuba in 1898, the United States blamed Cuba's ruler, Spain. In Saint Paul, Minnesota, seventeen-year-old Marjorie Bullard told her diary, "The Senate has had a terrible time deciding what to do and at last on Tuesday, April 19, Congress declared war [on Spain]."

Sarah Baylor wrote her thoughts in diary after diary. She thought of each diary as a friend. When one diary ended, she wrote, "I have finished my old diary. I hate to put it away as I just love the old worn cover." She closed by writing, "Goodbye dear old diary."

PACIFIC
OCEAN

N

CANADA

Washington

Oregon

Montana

North
Dakota

Idaho

Wyoming

South
Dakota

Nevada

Utah

Colorado

Nebraska

California

Kansas

Arizona

New
Mexico

Oklahoma

Texas

MEXICO

Boys and girls from an orphanage in Cincinnati, Ohio,
board a trolley in about 1910.

In some cities, people rode streetcars (also called trolleys) that ran
on tracks laid in the street. Trains roared along newly laid tracks
that crisscrossed the nation. And in October 1900, Wilbur and
Orville Wright made the first airplane flight. Youngsters began
dreaming of "flying machines" as another new way to get around.

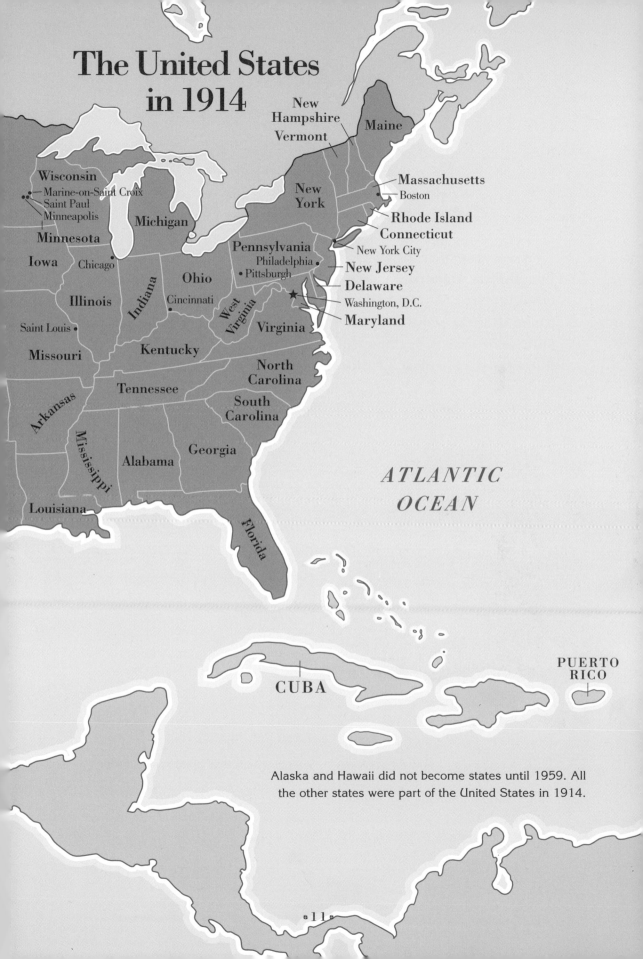

The United States in 1914

Wisconsin

Marine-on-Saint Croix
Saint Paul
Minneapolis
Minnesota

Michigan

Iowa   Chicago

Illinois

Indiana

Ohio

Cincinnati

Saint Louis

Missouri

Kentucky

West Virginia

Virginia

Arkansas

Tennessee

North Carolina

Mississippi

Alabama

Georgia

South Carolina

Louisiana

Florida

New Hampshire
Vermont
Maine

New York

Massachusetts
Boston

Rhode Island
Connecticut

Pennsylvania
Philadelphia
Pittsburgh

New York City

New Jersey

Delaware

Washington, D.C.

Maryland

ATLANTIC OCEAN

CUBA

PUERTO RICO

Alaska and Hawaii did not become states until 1959. All the other states were part of the United States in 1914.

THE CHILDREN'S HOUR

Between the dark and the daylight,
When the night is beginning to lower,
Comes a pause in the day's occupations,
That is known as the Children's Hour.

This verse is from a longer poem by Henry Wadsworth Longfellow. He wrote it about his three young daughters, who often interrupted his work. The poem describes the quiet time at the end of the workday when he and other fathers came home and spent time with their children. Most fathers in earlier times did not set aside time just for being fathers.

Just for Children

A popular saying at the turn of this new century was "Children should be seen but not heard." Wealthy parents hired nannies to

Young boys like Bradford Burris, *left*, and Charles Burris, *right*, wore dresses until about age five.

care for children. In these families, young children seldom ate with their parents. Instead, they ate in the nursery, a special room of the house just for children.

Adults in earlier centuries had depended on children to help with household chores and other hard work. As the 1900s began, many adults thought children should be free to be kids. Children in earlier times had owned few toys. But by 1900, stores were bursting with rocking horses, tin soldiers, dolls, and other toys made in factories. In the 1800s, children usually read books written for adults. By 1900 many books just for children had appeared.

Playgrounds became common in parks and at schools. The first amusement parks appeared. Young people squealed with delight on the Switchback Railway—a roller coaster ride at Coney Island in New York City. Trolley parks were similar. They were built by trolley companies at the edges of cities. Families took the trolley to these parks to ride the Ferris wheel, picnic, or row a rented boat around a pond.

No wonder people said the 1900s would be the century of the child. In a poem in one schoolbook, the poet longed to

Children on a jungle gym in New York City. The nation's first playgrounds appeared in the late 1800s.

"Backward, turn backward, O Time, in your flight. Make me a child again, Just for to-night!"
—*Elizabeth Akers Allen, 1896*

be a child again. "Backward, turn backward, / O Time, in your flight," she wrote. "Make me a child again, / Just for to-night!"

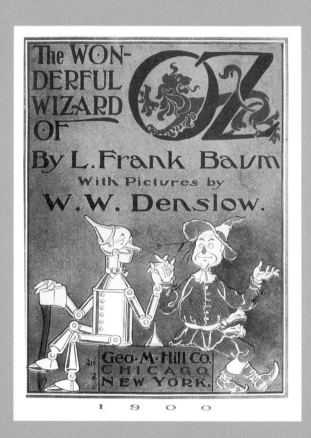

CHAPTER TWO

No Place Like Home

"*There is no place like home.*"

—Dorothy in The Wonderful Wizard of Oz, *a novel by L. Frank Baum, 1900*

❈ ❈

In L. Frank Baum's book *The Wonderful Wizard of Oz,* Dorothy, the heroine, has been whisked away to the fairy-tale land of Oz. She wishes with all her might to go home to Kansas. "No matter how dreary and grey our homes are, we people of flesh and blood would rather live there than in any other country," she said.

Children in the early 1900s lived in many different kinds of homes. Some children were rich, some were poor. Some lived in cities, some on farms. Most families were large. Children usually lived with both their mother and their father.

❈ ❈ ❈ ❈

In the White House

From 1901 to 1908, the United States had a popular, young president— Theodore Roosevelt. President Roosevelt's second son, Kermit, was eleven when his father became president. Kermit kept diaries for many years. The president traveled often and wrote his children warm, funny letters whenever he was away. The president's letters and Kermit's diaries tell a lot about the Roosevelt family.

No matter how busy the president was, he always made time for his children. Together they played blindman's bluff, had fierce pillow fights, and told ghost stories. A boy at heart, Roosevelt loved "scrambles" (hikes). Sometimes he pretended to be a "very big bear," growling and grunting. His children acted the parts of "little bears, raccoons, or badgers."

The Roosevelt family in 1903. *Left to right:* Quentin, President Roosevelt, Ted Jr., Archie, Alice, Kermit, Mrs. Roosevelt, and Ethel

Alice was the oldest child. She was followed by Ted Jr., Kermit, Ethel, Archie, and Quentin. The six children were supposed to behave properly in their elegant new home. But they still roller-skated in the halls, clumped around on stilts, and fenced using wooden sticks as swords. They were supposed to mind their manners during meals. But when cake was served, their father often slipped extra frosting onto their plates.

The Roosevelt youngsters brought many pets (including a raccoon, a kangaroo rat, squirrels, lizards, and twenty-one guinea pigs) to the White House. Seventeen-year-old Alice kept a pet snake named Emily Spinach. When Archie came down with measles and whooping cough, his brother Quentin smuggled Archie's pony, Algonquin, up to Archie's room. Archie soon felt better.

The Roosevelts also had a vacation home called Sagamore Hill. The children's favorite game there was an obstacle race in the barn. With their father holding the stopwatch, the children raced into the hayloft, out the window, and around the barn to the finish line.

❋ ❋ ❋ ❋

On the Baylor Plantation

Sarah Evelyn Baylor lived in a Virginia mansion called Staunton Hill. Sarah was eleven in 1895, when she told her diary that Staunton Hill was "a big white house with tall pillars and trees on each side." Vast flower gardens surrounded the house. The family kept horses and a carriage in a carriage house. In nearby fields, the Baylors grew hay and raised cows.

No photograph of Sarah Baylor's home exists, but it was large and comfortable like this Virginia plantation home.

Unlike many children at that time, Sarah had her own bedroom. It was roomy enough for her many clothes, a silk chair, and a fireplace. Servants did most of the household work and helped take care of Sarah.

Sarah liked to visit friends and relatives, paint, and grow flowers. She liked riding horses. When Sarah was thirteen, a neighbor man told Sarah's grandmother to forbid Sarah to ride a spirited horse. "Grandma let me do it," Sarah wrote in her diary. "I am not going to do like he says. Hateful old thing."

> *"I am not going to*
> *do like he says.*
> *Hateful old thing."*
> —*Sarah Evelyn Baylor, 1897*

On the Anderson Farm

George Anderson's parents were Jonas and Emma Sophia Anderson, Swedish immigrants who settled on a farm near Marine-on-Saint Croix, Minnesota. The family lived in a log cabin with an upstairs loft where the children slept.

Just 150 people lived in Marine-on-Saint Croix in the early 1900s. But like small towns all over the United States, it had a general store, a post office, a library, and a livery stable for horses.

George kept a diary telling about his everyday life. He helped his father milk cows every morning and night. In the warmth of the barn, with the smell of hay all around, father and son talked by the light of the kerosene lanterns. (Many homes in big cities had electricity in the early 1900s, but most farms didn't have electricity yet.)

After chores, George and his friends played catch. Sometimes they gathered at the train depot to watch the trains or to hop on a caboose for a short ride.

Other Kinds of Homes

In big city slums, poor families lived in crowded, rundown apartment buildings called tenements. A family of ten might live in one or two small rooms. Some rooms had peeling walls, leaky pipes, and no windows. Dark and airless, these homes looked like caves. Trash and sewage littered the streets, and rats skittered along.

Parents who worked sometimes left their youngest children at home with older children in charge. The older children became substitute parents who scrubbed floors and washed clothes while they minded the little ones.

Many Native Americans had European-style homes. Others lived in old-style homes. On the open plains, traditional Native Americans lived in tepees (cone-shaped tents made of animal hides or cloth stretched over poles). In the eastern woodlands, some

A New York City tenement apartment

A Cheyenne father and his children gather in front of their tepee. Most Native Americans at the turn of the last century were forced to live on reservations.

Native Americans built wigwams. Wigwams look like an upside-down half of a huge walnut shell. At night, Native American families gathered around the fire inside their tepee or wigwam to tell stories. When the fire burned low, everyone lay down, drew robes or blankets over themselves, and went to sleep.

Some children had no family. Their parents had died or couldn't care for them. Many of these children lived in orphanages. Beginning in 1854, the Children's Aid Society began looking for homes for these children out West. Adults from the society accompanied children as they traveled west by train. Between 1854 and 1929, some 200,000 children rode the orphan trains.

When a train carrying orphans chugged into town, a crowd gathered. Hopeful orphans waited for people in the crowd to choose them. A couple might pick a child because her face was sweet or because he looked like he would be a good worker. The child then went home with that family to live. Some children made several trips on an orphan train before finding a home.

❈ ❈ ❈ ❈

Sick Days

Children at the turn of this new century knew more about sickness and death than most modern children. Church bells tolled for a death. "The baptist bell tolled for somebody's death this afternoon,"

THE WHITE PLAGUE

Close to Christmas in 1907, a skinny newsboy in ragged clothes rushed into a Philadelphia newspaper building. The boy had read that people in the lobby were selling some special stamps. The money raised from the stamps would help fight the deadly disease tuberculosis. The boy plunked down a penny and said, "Gimme one—me sister's got it."

Tuberculosis killed 156,000 people in the United States in 1907—more than any other disease. It was called the white plague because people with tuberculosis looked so pale. The special stamps on sale were called Christmas seals. People could put the seals on letters and holiday cards along with regular postage. The American Lung Association still mails out Christmas seals every Christmas.

A little girl in a hospital for victims of the "white plague," tuberculosis, prays before bed.

In 1900 one-fourth of all American children died before age five.

wrote Eddie Longyear of Grass Lake, Michigan. "I think it was for Mr. Neufang's baby."

A century earlier, nearly one-half of all American children died before they reached the age of five. Many died from diseases such as scarlet fever and diphtheria. By 1900 one-fourth still died before age five. But most lived long enough to grow to adulthood.

One reason children were healthier was that people knew more about disease. Scientists had discovered that bacteria cause many diseases. People had also learned that clean food and water can prevent sickness.

This 1913 photograph shows people admiring the "Kentucky Sanitary Privy."
A privy was an outdoor toilet.

These children attended kindergarten at Hull-House in Chicago around 1900. Hull-House also offered classes to older children and adults, especially immigrants learning English as a second language.

Many Native Americans lived on reservations (land set aside for them). They were more likely to get "white men's diseases" such as smallpox, measles, and mumps. Among nonwhite children in 1900, more than one-third died before the age of five.

Reformer Jane Addams worked with children and adults in one poor neighborhood in Chicago. She founded Hull-House, a community center. People could take classes, get a meal, and even shower at Hull-House.

CHAPTER THREE

All
in a
Day's
Work

> ## *"Fixed up the window shades. Repaired everything imaginable. I am the right kind of boy."*
>
> *—George Anderson, January 6, 1900*

❋ ❋ ❋ ❋ ❋ ❋ ❋ ❋

In farm families like George Anderson's, being a good worker made children proud. They helped keep farms running. Even the smallest youngsters helped in the fields, picking up stones and breaking up dirt clumps. One Alabama

Opposite: Like generations of children before them, youngsters in the early 1900s helped their parents with chores such as milking cows. *Above*: George Anderson, *left*, and his brother Victor, *right*.

farmboy boasted that he could pick one hundred pounds of cotton a day by age eight. He pushed a plow bigger than he was.

Farm children also fed chickens, milked cows, and gathered eggs. Many loved their animals. Mary Goff, age twelve, named one newborn piglet Micah Hagar Sow. The piglet died when it was just three days old. "I buried her by a tree out in the grove," Mary wrote. "I felt awful bad and cried."

❋ ❋ ❋

Baking and Wash Day

In rich families, servants did household chores, but the children were still expected to help. Sarah Baylor, whose family had many

A boy with mop and pail. By 1900 many city homes had running water, and a new emphasis on cleanliness appeared.

servants, practiced baking every Saturday. Using her mother's new "beater," Sarah baked a sponge cake that turned out "very light," she wrote. Sarah's mother owned one of the country's most popular new appliances—a sewing machine. Sarah sewed doll clothes on it.

Middle-class children—whose parents worked as doctors, factory foremen, businessmen, or at other jobs—did chores, too. They mopped floors, cleaned windows, and pounded the dirt out of rugs with rug beaters. (Vacuum cleaners weren't invented until 1901.) They scrubbed walls soiled with soot from oil lamps.

In homes without running water or electricity, doing the laundry took all day. Youngsters beat the dirt out of clothes with a beater. They boiled white sheets and clothes on the stove in a big copper pot. Youngsters carried the wet laundry outside and hung it to dry on a clothesline. In cold weather, the clothes froze. "Taking the stiff frozen clothes off the lines was the most disagreeable part of laundering," one girl complained. Once icy clothes were brought back inside, they melted and dripped on the floor.

Working Children

Some poor children had real jobs. They labored in slaughterhouses (where animals were butchered), textile mills, coal mines, and many other places. In 1910 almost one-half of all children in the United States worked—two million in all.

From 1861 to 1865, Americans had fought the Civil War. After the war, all slaves, including children, were freed. By 1900 many former slaves and their children still lived in poverty. Some of these African American people farmed as sharecroppers who shared their profits with white landlords. Youngsters in these families had little time to learn or to play.

In coal-mining states, a ten-year-old boy might awake before dawn, ride an elevator down a dark mine shaft, and tend the mules that hauled coal. By the time the boy returned home, darkness had fallen.

Twelve-year-old Addie Laird working in a cotton mill in Pownal, Vermont, in 1910. No child labor laws protected children from long hours of work at the turn of the last century.

Boys working in a Pennsylvania coal mine. By the end of the day,
coal dust covered their faces and bodies.

Breaker boys sat hunched over a coal chute (shaft) built into the
side of a hill. As coal tumbled down the chute, they separated it
from worthless chunks of slate. Beginning at age eight or nine,
breaker boys worked from ten to sixteen hours each day. They often
suffered from cut fingers. Since they breathed coal dust all day long,
many got lung infections. Some boys chewed tobacco so they
wouldn't swallow coal dust.

In textile mills, children reached small fingers into whirring
machinery to repair snapped threads. They crawled under the
machines to oil them. Accidents happened. Children lost fingers,
even hands. In one ten-hour shift, a mill child might earn ten cents.
That much money didn't even buy a gallon of milk, which cost
twenty-seven cents in 1900.

Factory Work at Home

Many children worked for factories but did the work at home. In dingy apartments, children sewed cheap clothes, made lace and fake flowers, and strung beads. This kind of work was called piecework. Youngsters were paid for each piece completed. Some worked all day alongside their parents. Others worked after school.

In the 1890s, one widow and her daughters Mame, seven, and Jinny, six, made a living by sewing buttons on overalls. The girls' ragged clothes barely covered their thin bodies. Their hair stayed tangled and dirty. Their only toy was string leftover from binding the piles of overalls.

Some families rolled cigars for tobacco companies. Parents tightly rolled tobacco leaves into a cigar shape. Then children licked the cigar. Their spit held the leaves together. People didn't know that tobacco can cause dangerous illnesses. Some children licked as many as one thousand cigars each day.

An immigrant family does garment piecework in their New York City apartment. They are making feather decorations for hats—a fashion rage.

NEWSIES

On many city street corners, young boys called newsies sold newspapers, magazines, and other goods. To get customers interested in the papers, the boys often shouted out "Extra, Extra! Read All About It!"

Newsboys had to stand for long hours on street corners that were sometimes cold, wet, and dirty. In 1908 three thousand Boston newsboys decided to fight for better working conditions by forming an organization called the Newsboys' Republic. Members made rules for themselves and elected their own policemen and judges. One year they decided to change their own curfew from 10 P.M. to 8 P.M. That way newsies could quit work early without being pushed out of business by the competition.

Change on the March

No national law protected children from long hours of labor. Some states had child labor laws but didn't enforce them.

In 1903 a group of brave youngsters helped draw attention to the child labor problem. Four hundred children who worked in Philadelphia cotton mills followed reformer Mother Jones in a

Mother Jones with marchers. In 1903 young textile workers marched with her to President Roosevelt's home near New York City to demand the right to go to school.

march to President Roosevelt's Sagamore Hill home near New York City. Children playing fifes and drums led the long column of ragtag marchers. Other children carried signs saying "We Want To Go To School!" and "We Want Time To Play." Newspaper reports called this famous march the March of the Mill Children.

> *"No children in the mines and mills of the future is my cry."*
> —*Mother Jones, labor reformer, 1903*

Along the way, Mother Jones gave speeches about the evils of child labor. "We want President Roosevelt to hear the wail of the children who . . . work eleven and twelve hours a day in the textile mills," she said. "No children in the mines and mills of the future is my cry." Mother Jones and her followers demanded an end to child labor, but many years passed before their wish came true.

CHAPTER FOUR

The School Bell Rings

Children outside Square Lake School, 1893, near the Anderson farm in Minnesota. George Anderson, thirteen, is in the back row *(second from right)* with his brother Victor *(far right)*, eleven.

"At first I hated the school, but by and by I got so I could stand it."

—Huckleberry Finn, in The Adventures of Huckleberry Finn *by Mark Twain, 1884*

✿ ✿

In the early 1900s, most states didn't have laws that said children must go to school. Children who worked in mines, mills, and factories rarely went to school. Even so, more children attended school than ever before. Fifteen million children under the age of fourteen lived in the United States in 1900. Almost 75 percent of them attended school.

Two new kinds of schools became common. One kind was kindergarten, where five-year-olds played games and heard stories. (In earlier times, children waited longer before starting school.) High schools were also new.

✿ ✿ ✿ ✿

One-Room Schoolhouses

In 1900 the United States had 200,000 one-room schoolhouses. The teacher in a one-room schoolhouse taught children aged five to sixteen years old. The teacher worked with small groups while other students worked on their own or helped each other. A twelve-year-old might help an eight-year-old with math. A ten-year-old might teach a fourteen-year-old immigrant child to read in English.

In most schoolhouses, students perched on long benches. Other

Many classrooms in the early 1900s were heated by wood- or coal-burning stoves.

schools had desks. A potbelly stove warmed the room in winter. Since these schools had no bathrooms, an outhouse stood out back.

In the country, children often traveled several miles to get to school. They walked, rode on horseback, or clomped through snow on snowshoes. If the weather was bad, children stayed home. Teachers never knew if they would be working with five students or twenty-five.

Teachers taught whatever they knew. Some knew more than others did. Most taught the basics—reading, writing, and arithmetic. They used all-purpose textbooks called readers. *McGuffey's Eclectic Reader* and other readers contained stories, poems, plays, and lessons in speaking and spelling. Teachers disciplined children as needed. A mischievous child in a one-room schoolhouse might feel the sting of a hickory stick rapped across the knuckles.

Older students studied geography, nature, history, classic books, and grammar. Children memorized poems to recite. One popular poem was "The Village Blacksmith" by Henry Wadsworth Longfellow.

Children also learned how to write essays, give orations (speeches), argue in debates, and do experiments. Eddie Longyear, age eleven, remembered one activity. "Mr. Denison came in our room and showed us some experiments in electricity," Eddie wrote. "I took three shocks."

WHAT TO DO AT SCHOOL

One book listed the following rules for youngsters
to follow at school:

*Don't forget to take off your cap when you
enter school.*

*Don't forget to say "Good Morning" to your
teacher.*

Don't worry your schoolmates with tricks.

Don't whistle in school.

*Don't forget to brush your clothes, comb your
hair, and polish your shoes before going to
school.*

*Don't forget to raise your hat if you meet your
teacher or any other teacher on the street.*

*Don't (This is for girls particularly) giggle—
laugh, but not too loud.*

Don't chew the corners of your handkerchief.

—from *Polite Manners for Little Men and Women*,
Daphne Dale, 1911

Mary Goff went to a one-room schoolhouse in central Minnesota. She mailed many of her school essays to contests in magazines such as *Farm, Stock, and Home*. On a spring day in 1899, Mary got good news in the mail. Her essay "An April Adventure" had won a prize.

❋ ❋ ❋ ❋

City Schools

City schools were much larger than country schools. City schools divided students into grades. Each grade had a separate classroom. Slate chalkboards lined the beige or cream walls. (Educators thought bright colors were bad for children's eyes and brains.) Identical desks with uncomfortable benches attached were arranged in perfect rows. Children sat up straight. Unruly boys who sat behind girls dipped their long braids into the inkwells sunk into each desk.

A few city schools were spacious, well lighted, and comfortable. Children studied up-to-date textbooks. But most city schools overflowed with children. School leaders sometimes had to turn office buildings and warehouses into dark, stuffy classrooms. In crowded neighborhoods, children went to school in shifts, morning or afternoon.

❋ ❋ ❋ ❋

Private Boarding Schools

Many wealthy youngsters attended private boarding schools. Living away from home, they grew especially close to their school chums. In 1903 Kermit Roosevelt attended an exclusive private school called Groton. He gave his Groton friends these nicknames: Phin, Pieface, Hippo, Donk, Duffer, and Shrimp. Kermit looked forward to getting letters from his father. Whenever Kermit got discouraged and homesick, President Roosevelt tried to cheer him up. "Blessed Kermit," the president wrote one day. "Don't worry about the

THOSE ROOSEVELT RASCALS

Quentin and Archie Roosevelt attended Force Public School, an elementary school in Washington, D.C. The boys frequently got into trouble for misdeeds such as tossing erasers. Once Quentin fired a spitball at a classmate but hit the teacher instead. She hauled Quentin off to the coatroom for a scolding. The next morning, President Roosevelt appeared at school with flowers for her. The president apologized for his son, saying he hoped Quentin had learned a lesson. But several years passed before the Roosevelt boys stopped getting into trouble at school.

Quentin Roosevelt

lessons, old boy. I know you are studying hard. Don't get cast down." When it was time for Kermit to pack his trunk to go home for a holiday , he wrote, "The trunks are down [from the attic]. Hurrah! Hurrah! Hurrah!"

Home Schooling

Sarah Evelyn Baylor did most of her early schooling at home. As some modern parents do, Sarah's mother taught her own children to read and write. Good penmanship was an important skill for children in the early 1900s. Sarah practiced her handwriting by writing practice sentences over and over in lined copybooks. One day's practice sentence was "Writing is almost as important as speaking." Sarah also loved reading. Two of her favorite books were *Little Women* by Louisa May Alcott and *David Copperfield* by Charles Dickens.

STINK POTS

One day in 1903, Kermit Roosevelt was sick and had to go to the school infirmary. He complained about some strong-smelling stuff that nurses were simmering in a pot. The stinky stuff was supposed to help them get better. "Is there anything worse than this staying in the infirmary . . . with temperature of 85 degrees and an awful 'stink pot' which nearly stifles you?" he wrote. Kermit and the other patients got in trouble for hiding the stink pot in the chimney.

Equal Education for All

At the time, educators such as Horace Mann thought every American child should get an equal education. That hardly ever happened,

A school for African American children in the southern United States. Schools for African American children were more crowded and had fewer supplies than schools for white children.

Red Lake Boarding School, 1915. The U.S. government took many Native American children from their homes and forced them to learn "white men's ways" at boarding schools like this one in Red Lake, Minnesota.

though. In many states, white and black children went to separate schools. Schools for white children received ten times as much government money as schools for black children did.

Some states had high schools for white children but none for black children. White colleges refused to admit black students. In 1881 in Alabama, reformer Booker T. Washington founded the first college for black students, Tuskegee Institute.

The education of Native American children was unequal, too. By 1890 many were forced to go to government boarding schools or to schools run by the Catholic Church. These schools were nothing like the boarding schools of the rich. Indian children had no choice about being separated from their families. They were forbidden to speak their native language at school. School staff members cut the children's long hair and forced them to wear the clothing white children wore. The U.S. government expected school to replace home and family for these children.

CHAPTER FIVE

Just for Fun

"Do you believe in fairies? Say quick that you believe! If you believe, clap your hands!"

—*James M. Barrie*, Peter Pan: Or the Boy Who Would Not Grow Up, *1905*

A new play called *Peter Pan* opened in the United States in 1905. It told the story of Peter, the boy who never grows up. His friend, a tiny fairy named Tinker Bell, is going to die unless the children in the Darling family believe in her. As real children watched this play, the actor playing Peter asked them to help. "If you believe [in fairies]," he said, "clap your hands! Don't let Tinker Bell die!" Children in the audience clapped and clapped. Later the author turned the play into a book.

The early 1900s brought plenty of magic fun into people's lives. Theater companies and vaudeville troupes traveled to small towns all over the nation. They delighted everyone with their comedy skits, magic shows, and song-and-dance routines. When a traveling circus rolled into town, children watched clowns and acrobats perform under a "big top" tent.

A new and exciting kind of entertainment arrived in 1889—motion pictures. Thomas Edison, the famous inventor of the electric lightbulb, also invented the movie camera. The first movies had no sound. Sometimes a piano player played live music to match a movie's mood. The pictures flickered so much that movies were sometimes called flickering flicks.

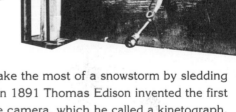

Opposite: Youngsters make the most of a snowstorm by sledding down the street. *Right:* In 1891 Thomas Edison invented the first movie camera, which he called a kinetograph.

Ring-a-Ring-a-Rosy

Children all over the country loved games. When Ojibwe (Anishinaabe) Indian children played hide-and-seek, they drew

Playing marbles was a favorite pastime at the turn of the last century.

long and short sticks to see who would cover their eyes first. Whoever was "It" sang "Butterfly, butterfly, show me where to go!" while the other children hid.

All kinds of children ran races, walked fences, and played marbles. Group singing games like ring-a-ring-a-rosy had simple rules and took little or no equipment. Youngsters fished in streams or hunted for squirrels, grouse, or quail. One day, Sarah Baylor wrote that she had collected "two hats full" of strawberries.

Baseball became a favorite national sport, especially when the American League baseball organization formed in 1900 and the first World Series followed in 1903. Young people began riding trolleys to see professional teams such as the Brooklyn Dodgers. Ordinary people also played baseball in small towns and cities and on ranches and farms. Thousands of city children played the street form of baseball, stickball.

In cold climates, children rode toboggans and ice skated. One cold Thanksgiving Day in Minnesota in 1892, Maude Maguire's younger brother Allie spent seven hours ice skating. Cold didn't bother Kermit Roosevelt

Baseball became a popular sport in the early 1900s.

either. "I froze my feet at hockey, and had a tremendous time melting them," he wrote in January 1908.

Kermit and his friends often held water pistol fights in their Groton dormitory. They also played cops and robbers in the gym. Eddie Longyear and his pal Sherdie loved to fish and swim. Eddie also liked playing the drum his uncle had given him.

> *"I froze my feet at hockey, and had a tremendous time melting them."*
>
> —Kermit Roosevelt, 1908

Teddy Bears and Shoo Fly Rocking Horses

Marbles, kites, checkers, and balls had been popular for many years. But by 1900, factories were turning out wonderful and affordable toys such as spinning tops, jack-in-the-boxes, steam-driven train sets, and dancing dolls called marionettes. The 1902 Sears, Roebuck, & Co. Catalog included "Boys' Steel Wagons" ($1.50), "Shoo Fly Rocking Horses" ($1.08), a "Dressed Sailor Doll" ($.25), and a "Horseman's Box Kite" ($.17).

A timeless toy became popular in 1902. During a hunting trip, President Roosevelt caught a wild bear cub. Instead of killing it, Roosevelt spared its life. The owner of a New York toy shop soon began selling "Teddy's Bear," a cuddly toy bear with button eyes. Children everywhere suddenly wanted their own teddy bear.

A "teddy bear." Teddy bears were named after the nation's popular president Teddy Roosevelt.

Some parents bought their children educational toys. Cast-iron banks with moving parts were both toys and reminders to children to save money. When a coin was popped into one of these banks, the coin set the bank in motion. Parents thought that dominoes and building blocks developed children's logic skills. Crayola® crayons also became popular.

Rolling hoops was a popular pastime. Anyone could make a hoop from an old buggy wheel or automobile wheel. To push a hoop along, a youngster attached a skimmer (a straight piece of wire) to the center of the hoop.

Although girls and boys played many of the same games, parents often encouraged them to choose different play activities. Boys staged battles with toy soldiers. They also made buildings out of Lincoln logs and erector sets and raced their toy cars, trucks, and trains. Such toys supposedly got boys ready to be men. Native American boys played with bows and arrows, pretending they were hunting and fishing.

Dolls helped girls practice to be mothers and homemakers. Store-bought dolls were beautiful, with delicate heads of porcelain, china, or wax. Ringlets made of human hair framed doll faces. Dolls often came with houses to live in, plus carriages, tea sets, wardrobes, watches, and tiny hot water bottles. Some girls made their own dolls from socks, handkerchiefs, and even cucumbers and cornhusks.

Mary Wigginton's doll, Gertrude. Gertrude has a delicate wax face, real human hair, and a stylish coat with black velvet bows.

"I Shall Tell You a Story"

Toward the end of the 1800s, parents began to believe that reading made children happy. Sarah Baylor eagerly watched the mail for issues of *St. Nicholas*, a magazine just for children. It had stories and rhymes, riddles, a "How To Do and Make" section, and chapters from books. Books such as Frances Hodgson Burnett's *Little Lord Fauntleroy* and Louisa May Alcott's *Jo's Boys* were popular. Rudyard Kipling's *Jungle Book*, published in 1894, became a much-loved children's book.

Books just for children were rare until the turn of the last century.

Around 1900 a British author named Beatrix Potter wrote a letter to a small boy named Noel. "I don't know what to write to you," she said, "so I shall tell you a story about four little rabbits whose names were Flopsy, Mopsy, Cottontail, and Peter." Beatrix Potter's story became a popular book, *The Tale of Peter Rabbit*. In other Beatrix Potter books, children fell in love with Peter Rabbit, Squirrel Nutkin, and Mrs. Tiggle-Winkle. These small books fit perfectly into a young child's hands.

Holidays

Many people celebrated special holidays in winter. At Christmastime in December, toys and ornaments dangled from the ceilings of country stores. Treasures glittered behind the plate glass windows of city shops. Most people who celebrated Christmas had a tree that

Factories turned out beautiful toys, but most were expensive. Many children received simple handmade gifts during the winter holidays.

glowed with lighted candles. Some families lit their trees with a popular new invention—strings of electric lights. People decorated their trees with bags of candies, small toys, glass ornaments, paper chains, and strings of cranberries or popcorn.

Christmas and Hanukkah gifts were often practical, such as hand-knit socks or wool ties. In Michigan, Eddie Longyear's gifts one Christmas were more fancy. He got a box of dominos, a book, a necktie, a boot-shaped pincushion, candy, and thirty-five cents. "Quite a number!" Eddie told his diary.

On the first day of May, many schoolchildren danced around a maypole (a tall pole with ribbons streaming down from the top). Each child held one of the ribbons. Then the group circled the pole. Every other child went in one direction. The rest went in the other direction. Soon the ribbons looked like a woven plait (a braid). This tradition was called "plaiting the maypole."

In many towns, the most festive day of the year was the Fourth of July. Farm families decorated their horses and wagons and drove to town. City folks watched as brass bands played and marched in parades. Youngsters stuffed themselves with fried chicken, lemonade, and the new rage, ice cream cones. After dark came the fireworks.

THE NIGHT BEFORE CHRISTMAS

In 1822 Clement Clarke Moore wrote "A Visit from Saint Nicholas," a poem based on the legend of a jolly elf who brought toys to children at Christmas. The poem introduced Saint Nicholas to many children around the world. By 1900 many children in the United States knew about the American version of Saint Nicholas, Santa Claus. Moore's poem came to be called "The Night before Christmas" (the poem's first line).

In 1897 one little girl wrote to the *New York Sun* newspaper to ask this question about Santa Claus:

Dear Editor:

I am eight years old. Some of my little friends say there is no Santa Claus. Papa says "If you see it in The Sun, it's so." Please tell the truth: Is there a Santa Claus?

Virginia O'Hanlon

The newspaper editor wrote back: "Yes, Virginia, there is a Santa Claus."

FIRE CRACKERS

One year Mary Goff and her friends celebrated the Fourth of July in the town of Easton, Minnesota. "After tramping the streets of Easton till toward night, . . . we blew off roman candles, sky rockits, spinning wheels, fire crakers, etc.," Mary told her diary.

A family celebrates the Fourth of July in Saint Paul, Minnesota, in 1911.

On Halloween night, children didn't get treats. But older children pulled pranks and tricks. Young pranksters rang doorbells, shot peas at houses with peashooters, hung garbage cans on poles, or moved outhouses. Some boys in George Anderson's town lifted a buggy and put it on top of a shed.

Birthdays were also special times. When Sarah Baylor's sister Annie turned nine in 1896, Sarah gave Annie a small case for keeping needles. When Annie's party guests played one game, they won prizes. Sarah listed some of the prizes in her diary: "a pretty little red book with a glass picture on it, a lovely brass pin tray . . . and a little knife." Later, the birthday guests played lawn croquet until a carriage came to take them home.

Dressed for Fun

People dressed up in this era, even for summer picnics. The men wore coats, ties, and hats. Women and girls wore airy white dresses. Little girls wore straw hats and loose dresses with black stockings underneath.

As in earlier times, young people were supposed to dress modestly. But by the early 1900s, many girls wore bloomers for active sports like bicycle riding. Bloomers (baggy trousers under a knee-length skirt) worked better than long skirts for this popular new sport. Sixteen-year-old Polly Bullard shortened the hem of an old gray skirt so that it skimmed the top of her boots, making it "the right length for bicycle-riding."

Even on hot days, young people usually wore plenty of clothes. When Sarah Baylor went barefoot one summer day, she said that shedding her shoes was "a great privilege." A boy's bathing suit looked like long underwear. Girls swam in suits that looked like dresses and covered them to the knees. The suits were often made of wool, which grew heavy in the water.

One day in 1903, when Kermit Roosevelt and his friends wanted to go swimming, they decided that they didn't need bathing suits. Sensibly waiting until "after the girls and ladies left," the boys went skinny-dipping.

Older girls and young women shortened their long skirts to ankle length as a bicycle riding craze swept the nation.

CHAPTER SIX

Betwixt Twelve and Twenty

"In the end she grew up of her own free

Between the ages of twelve and twenty, young people had more responsibilities than when they had been little. But they had more freedom, too. Some young people had already left school and were working by age thirteen. Other teenagers went on to high school and then to college. Many older teens married.

Older boys and girls often did things together, just as modern teens do. George Anderson wrote about a gathering with his friends in January 1900. "Supper at 7, games till 12 . . . all rode in a lumber wagon . . . plaid [played] all kinds of games." George and his friends played one card game called whist. George never told his grandmother, since she called card playing the "work of the devil."

In the country, friends and neighbors often lived miles apart. Telephone calls were expensive, so people mailed invitations for get-togethers. The sender then waited for a written reply. George Anderson wrote some of his friends on leather postcards using one-cent stamps. Young people looked forward to picking up the mail as much as modern teens enjoy talking on the phone or checking their e-mail. When friends came over, they often gathered around the piano or the pianola (a piano that played by itself).

Opposite: A mother and daughter at the piano together.
Right: A telephone from around 1900. Often several neighbors shared one telephone line. They could eavesdrop on each other's conversations just by picking up the phone.

will a day quicker than other girls."

—*from* Peter Pan *by J. M. Barrie, speaking of Wendy, the oldest Darling child*

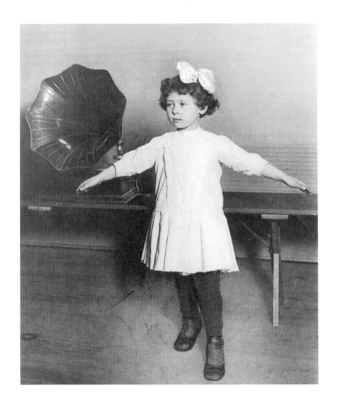

On this gramophone, the flowerlike horn is broadcasting the sound, just as modern speakers do for sound systems.

Parents wanted their children to learn to play the piano. Mary Goff's mother even promised to buy Mary a gold ring if Mary would practice. One popular type of piano music was a kind of jazz known as ragtime. "Maple Leaf Rag" by Scott Joplin became a famous ragtime tune.

A wind-up machine called a gramophone played tunes recorded on round, unbreakable disks. These records were ten inches wide, much larger than CDs or DVDs. One ad promised that the gramophone was "the greatest entertainment of the age."

※ ※ ※ ※

Box Socials and Dancing

Young people often gathered at "box socials." Before the event, girls packed lunch for two in a decorated box or basket. Then an auctioneer at the social held up each box. Boys bid for the one they wanted. Boxes weren't marked, but sometimes a girl told a special boy which lunch was hers.

Other gatherings where young people mingled were teas, concerts, and sporting events. At an ice skating party in 1908, Kermit Roosevelt took special notice of one young woman, Carrie. She was "very pretty and attractive," he told his diary.

Young people danced whenever they could. In 1892 Maude Maguire lived at a boarding school in Minnesota. "Every girl in the school dances and takes lessons," she wrote. "Even the smallest girls can dance splendidly." When the girls at Maude's school joined the boys at a nearby military academy for dances, adult chaperones watched closely. "We can't turn around without encountering one or more teachers," Maude complained. "But some of the girls always manage to find a secluded spot [to be alone with a boy]."

> *"Every girl in the school dances and takes lessons. Even the smallest girls can dance splendidly."*
> —*Maude Maguire, 1892*

Raising a Ruckus in the White House

President Teddy Roosevelt's oldest daughter, Alice, was seventeen in 1901. Daring, headstrong, and full of fun, Alice often slid down White House banisters. Once she landed in the middle of an important presidential conversation. She also smoked cigarettes, played tennis in short skirts, and bet on racehorses. Many considered her behavior improper. But her father claimed, "I can be President of the United States—or—I can attend to Alice." He couldn't do both.

President Roosevelt sent Alice on two trips as a good will ambassador for the United States. She went to Puerto Rico in 1903 when she was nineteen. Two years later, she traveled to the Far East and met with leaders of Japan, China, Korea, the Philippines, and other countries. Everybody loved reading about Alice's trips in the

Alice Roosevelt in about 1906. Alice wasn't quiet and sweet, as girls were supposed to be. Instead, she spoke her mind, traveled around the world, and got in trouble for driving fast.

newspapers. Reporters called the Far East trip "Alice in Wonderland."

Because Alice wore elegant fashions, people nicknamed her Princess Alice. Girls copied her styles. When Alice announced that her favorite color was blue-gray, the color became a fad. A song called "Alice Blue Gown" was an instant hit.

In earlier times, girls were supposed to look fragile. But Alice had the perfect figure and fashionable clothes of a new American ideal, the Gibson girl. The name came from the drawings of illustrator Charles Dana Gibson, who drew fresh, athletic-looking young women. Gibson girls wore sporty blouses called shirtwaists and simple, flared skirts. This outfit looked comfortable, but it still demanded that a girl have a waist as narrow as a wasp's. So girls laced their corsets as tightly as they could.

Alice's brother Kermit also raised a ruckus in the White House. On December 31, 1908, he and his friends celebrated the New Year by dancing on the White House roof. "We had a grand large supper. . . . I rushed [flirted with] Carrie," nineteen-year-old Kermit gleefully told his diary. After supper they danced on the roof "until Father and Mother heard and quickly stopped [us]. . . . Then the girls went to bed and we [boys] raided the pantry!"

Getting Serious

Just as in earlier times, many girls went straight from girlhood to marriage. When boys and girls kept steady company with marriage in mind, they were "courting." Courting couples held hands, kissed, danced, and wrote letters to each other.

Young people usually married in their late teens or early twenties. By age fourteen, Maude Maguire had already started to worry about becoming an old maid (a woman who never married). She thought that would be "quite a joke on me," as she wrote in her diary in 1893. On the other hand, "I think some old maids real nice." By 1900 about 20 percent of American women (single and married) worked outside the home. Many became teachers, seamstresses, or secretaries. Some worked in mills and factories.

Frederick Wigginton was in his twenties when he moved from England to the United States. He left behind his sweetheart, Gertrude Livock. They stayed in touch by writing letters. Their letters took three weeks to

"I think some old maids real nice."

—*Maude Maguire, 1893*

A Gibson Girl and her sweetheart

A SONG ABOUT SWEETHEARTS

*You were my queen
in calico,*

*I was your bashful,
barefoot beau,*

*And you wrote on
my slate,*

"I love you Joe,"

*When we were a
couple of kids.*

*—from "School Days,"
a popular song by
Will D. Cobb and Gus
Edwards, 1907*

travel across the Atlantic Ocean by ship. In one letter, Frederick told Gertrude that he was afraid the distance would come between them. She might find somebody else. "How could I," she wrote back, "when I was always thinking of you?"

On August 15, 1909, Frederick mailed Gertrude a special letter. "You see Gertie, it's like this," he wrote. "I have come to the conclusion that you are the only girl for me in this world, and I want your consent to an engagement between us."

Frederick had already asked Gertrude's mother for permission to marry her (her father had died). When Frederick finally received his answer, six weeks after sending his proposal, the news was good. Gertrude said yes. She traveled to the United States, where the two married in 1910.

Getting Married

As in modern times, some weddings were simple. Only the couple and witnesses attended. Other weddings were fancy. Many brides bought not only a beautiful wedding dress but also a trousseau (a complete wardrobe of new clothes for her new life as a wife). When Sarah Baylor's cousin Sally married in 1895, Sarah told her diary about her cousin's lovely new dresses. "The prettiest [was] a pink silk trimmed with lace with pink gause [gauze] over it," she wrote. It had "a lovely silk cape trimed [trimmed] with white fur."

In 1906 Alice Roosevelt married U.S. congressman Nicholas Longworth, who later became speaker of the House of Representatives. Their glamorous wedding took place at the White House. Wedding guests included important legislators and other famous people.

A bride cuts her wedding cake. Girls were expected to marry and start a family by their early twenties.

But Alice Roosevelt still insisted on doing things her way. Instead of having bridesmaids, she surrounded herself with groomsmen.

Memory Books

Many teenagers kept memory books, a type of scrapbook. Polly Bullard was fifteen when she told her diary what a memory book was. "It is a blank-book originally," she wrote, "and you paste in party favors, clippings from the newspapers, anything you wish, to remind you of your good times."

Marjorie Bullard, Polly's older sister, saved the memories of a special outing on June 21, 1896. She and her friends had traveled by streetcar and horse and buggy to a country farm. They had spent a day exploring, playing games, and eating. "Just before going home," Marjorie wrote later, "many of the girls that have memory books, went around hunting for things to put in them. . . . I brought an oak-leaf, a wisp of hay, a bit of asparagus, and a little piece of an evergreen."

> *"Just before going home, many of the girls that have memory books, went around hunting for things to put in them."*
> —*Marjorie Bullard, 1896*

Forget Me Not

The children in this book eventually grew up, as most children do. Sarah Baylor stopped keeping a diary after a while, so we have no record of her later life. Other children kept up their diaries. Mary Goff became a teacher in a one-room schoolhouse. Eddie Longyear went to college and studied engineering. Kermit Roosevelt became a soldier and then a businessman. Mary, Eddie, and Kermit all married and had children. George Anderson was too busy helping

Children wave good-bye to a passing train in Lindstrom, Minnesota. Children of this era also waved good-bye to an old century and became the first generation of the 1900s.

run the family farm to go to high school. He never married. Alice Roosevelt Longworth had one daughter, Paulina. Alice eventually met every president from William McKinley to Gerald Ford and lived to be ninety-six.

When George Anderson turned thirteen in 1894, he was given a velvet autograph book. Each guest at his birthday party wrote in the book. Olivia Osberg signed this way:

To My Friend George.
There is a small and simple flower
That twines around the humblest cot,
And in the sad and lonely hours,
It whispers low:"Forget me not."

Activities

Study Historical Illustrations

Nearly all the photographs in this book were made near the turn of the last century. They are black and white, since color photography wasn't in general use until the 1940s.

Old photographs give many clues about life in the past. Look at the photograph on page 32. It shows George Anderson (back row, second from the right) and his classmates in front of their school near Marine-on-Saint Croix, Minnesota. George is about thirteen years old. On his right is his brother Victor, age eleven.

Working with a partner, look at the details in the photo. Make a list of things you notice about the schoolhouse. How is it the same or different from your school? Next, study the children. What do you notice about their clothes and hairstyles? Which person do you think is the teacher?

Continue to ask questions as you study other photographs and illustrations in this book. Who are the people? Where are they? What are they doing? Who made the photograph or illustration and why?

Play Fox-and-Geese

Fox-and-geese was a popular game in 1900. To play, start by drawing the shape of a large wheel outside. Draw with a stick in the dirt or with chalk on a large paved surface. You could also tramp the circle in snow. Give the wheel four to six spokes. Then choose one person to be Fox. The other players are geese. Fox stands at the center (or hub) of the wheel as the geese line up along the wheel's spokes and rim, which are called rivers. Fox calls out, "Run, geese, run," and starts to chase the geese. Geese have to stay on the rivers. When a goose is tagged, he or she becomes Fox. Places where the lines intersect are safe bases.

Behave Yourself

Look at the school rules on page 35 from *Polite Manners for Little Men and Women* (1911). What are some of the rules at your school? How are they the same or different from the rules in *Polite Manners for Little Men and Women*? What would children living one hundred years ago have thought of your school's rules? What might someone one hundred years in the future think?

Pretend that you can send a letter to one of the children in this book. Write to him or her, explaining what your school is like. Be sure to explain the modern things you might mention, such as what a computer is.

Make a Memory Book

Find a notebook. Then take a hike, a bike ride, or some other outing. Gather little mementos like Polly Bullard did on page 58. Your mementos could include a leaf, a bird's feather, a postcard, or other things. Make notes in your notebook about your thoughts. Tell what you are seeing and feeling. When you get back, paste your mementos in your book alongside your notes. Your memory book could become a primary source someday, so be sure to sign and date it.

Make an Old-Fashioned Snack

Many girls at the turn of the last century learned how to cook at an early age. Some favorite recipes were sponge cake, johnnycake, ladyfingers, macaroons, caramel cake, sugar cookies, apple brown betty, fudge, and gingersnaps. People often made "water ices" with lemonade and other fruit juices. Several of the children in this book wrote in their diaries about making homemade lemonade, water ices, and bread-and-butter sandwiches. Modern boys and girls will enjoy this recipe.

Lemonade Water Ice

8 cups water · grated peel of 1 lemon

juice of 8 large lemons · (or 1 teaspoon store-bought lemon peel)

4 cups sugar

Use a hand squeezer (or an electric squeezer, a modern tool) to squeeze the juice of the lemons into a large pitcher. Add the other ingredients and stir. Pour the lemonade into ice cube trays and freeze. Then grind the frozen lemon cubes in a blender. Serve frosty cold.

Source Notes

6 Robert Louis Stevenson, "Happy Thought," *A Child's Garden of Verses* (1913; reprint, Oxford, England: Oxford University Press, 1996), 6–7.

7 Mary Wigginton [Reminisces of the author's mother], Encinitas, CA.

9 George Anderson, [Diary], December 31, 1899, Encinitas, CA: author's private collection.

9 Sarah Evelyn Courtney Baylor Blackford, [Diaries], April 1, 1897, and August 8, 1897, Mss. B5645b14, Box 14. Richmond, VA: Virginia Historical Society.

9 Marjorie L. Bullard, [Journal], April 24, 1897, Ms. A-B935A, St. Paul, MN: Minnesota Historical Society Manuscript Collection.

12 Henry Wadsworth Longfellow, "The Children's Hour," *The Atlantic Monthly*, September 1860.

13 Elizabeth Akers Allen, "Rock Me to Sleep," *McGuffey's Fifth Eclectic Reader* (1896; reprint, New York: John Wiley & Sons, 1997), 286.

15 L. Frank Baum, *The Wonderful Wizard of Oz* (1900; reprint, London, England: Octopus Books, 1981), 31.

15–16 Joan Paterson Kerry, *A Bully Father: Theodore Roosevelt's Letters to His Children* (New York: Random House, 1995), 49.

17 Sarah Baylor Blackford, July 9, 1895.

18 Ibid., August 7, 1897.

20–21 Edmund Joseph Longyear, [Diary], January 13, 1877, St. Paul, MN: Minnesota Historical Society.

22 Kathleen Doyle, "'Stamping' out Tuberculosis: The Story of Christmas Seals," *American History Illustrated*, November/December 1989, 66.

25 George Anderson, January 6, 1900.

25 Mary Goff, [Diary], n.d., Blue Earth, MN: Blue Earth Historical Society.

26–27 Henry William Herman Kolshorn and Mary Dorothy Teitge, [Kolshorn Family History], n.d., St. Paul, MN: Minnesota Historical Society.

31 Mother Jones, quoted in Judith Pinkerton Josephson, *Mother Jones: Fierce Fighter for Workers' Rights* (Minneapolis, MN: Lerner Publications Company, 1997), 86–87.

31 Philip Foner, *Mother Jones Speaks: Collected Writings and Speeches* (New York: Monad Press, 1983), 91–93.

33 Mark Twain, *Adventures of Huckleberry Finn* (1884; reprint, New York: Buccaneer Books, 1976), 11.

34 Edmund Joseph Longyear, n.d.

35 Daphne Dale, *Polite Manners for Little Men and Women* (No place of publication: Hamming, Publisher, 1911), 39–40.

36–37 Theodore Roosevelt, quoted in Kerry, 74.

37 Kermit Roosevelt, [Diary], December 15, 1903, Kermit and Belle Roosevelt Papers, Washington, D.C.: Library of Congress.

38 Kermit Roosevelt, January 19, 1903.

40 James M. Barrie, *Peter Pan: Or the Boy Who Would Not Grow Up* (first performed in London, England, 1904; New York: Charles Scribner's Sons, 1928).

41 Susan Bivin Aller, *J. M. Barrie: The Magic behind Peter Pan* (Minneapolis, MN: Lerner Publications Company, 1994), 7.

42 Sarah Baylor Blackford, Mary 22, 1895.

43 Kermit Roosevelt, January 31, 1908.

45 Beatrix Potter, quoted in Margaret Lane, *The Tale of Beatrix Potter* (Glasgow, Scotland: William Collins, 1968), introduction.

46 Edmund Joseph Longyear, January 8, 1878.

47 Virginia O'Hanlon, [letter to editor Francis P. Church and his reply], *New York Sun*, September 21, 1897.

48 Mary Goff, July 4, 1899.

48   Sarah Baylor Blackford, March 20, 1895.

49   Polly Caroline Bullard, [Reminiscencees and diary], May 23, 1897, Mss. CCT.B-935A, St. Paul, MN: Minnesota Historical Society.

49   Sarah Baylor Blackford, July 28, 1895.

49   Kermit Roosevelt, July 5, 1903.

50–51 Barrie.

51   George Anderson, January 1900.

53   Kermit Roosevelt, January 8, 1908.

53   Maude Maguire, [Papers], September 16, 1892, Ms. PP1760, St. Paul, MN: Minnesota Historical Society Manuscript Collection.

53   Theodore Roosevelt, quoted in Kerry, 70.

54   Kermit Roosevelt, July 5, 1903.

55   Maude Maguire, February12, 1893.

56   Will D. Cobb (lyrics), "School Days" (New York: Gus Edwards Publishing, 1907).

56   Gertrude Livock, letter to Frederick Wigginton, September 9, 1909, and Frederick Wigginton, letter to Gertrude Livock, August 15, 1909, Encinitas, CA: author's private collection.

57   Sarah Baylor Blackford, August 22, 1895.

58   Polly Bullard, August 22, 1895.

58   Marjorie Bullard, June 21, 1896.

59   George Anderson, [personal "memory book"], 1894, Encinitas, CA: author's private collection.

Selected Bibliography

Crichton, Judy. America *1900: The Turning Point*. New York: Henry Holt, 1998.

Jennings, Peter and Todd Brewster. *The Century*. New York: Doubleday, 1998.

Kerry, Joan Paterson. *A Bully Father: Theodore Roosevelt's Letters to His Children*. New York: Random House, 1995.

Rae, Noel, editor. *Witnessing America*. New York: Stonesong Press, 1996.

Sears, Stephen W., and the editors of American Heritage. *Hometown U.S.A*. New York: American Heritage Publishing, 1975.

West, Elliott. *Growing Up in Twentieth-Century America: A History and Reference Guide*. Westport, CT: Greenwood Press, 1996.

Further Reading & Websites

Abilock, Debbie, and Cynthia Hirsch Kosut. "Turn-of-the-Century Child." Library of Congress American Memory Fellows Program.
<http://nunuevaschool.org/~debbie/library/cur/20c/turn.html>.

Edge, Laura B. *A Personal Tour of Hull-House*. Minneapolis, MN: Lerner Publications Company, 2001.

Feldman, Ruth. *Don't Whistle in School*. Minneapolis, MN: Lerner Publications Company, 2001.

Freedman, Russell. *Kids at Work: Lewis Hine and the Crusade against Child Labor*. New York: Clarion Books, 1998.

Josephson, Judith Pinkerton. *Mother Jones: Fierce Fighter for Workers Rights*. Minneapolis, MN: Lerner Publications Company, 1998.

"Progressive Era to New Era, 1900–1929." Library of Congress Learning Page.
<http://memory.loc.gov/ammem/ndlpedu/features/timeline/progres.html>.

"Rise of Industrial America, 1876–1900." Library of Congress Learning Page.
<http://memory.loc.gov/ammem/ndlpedu/features/timeline/riseind.html>.

Index